sand cast

wayne turiansky

north atlantic books
plainfield, vermont

for meryl

I created eternity
To bind you within it
A scheme worthy of the pope
To keep my prince

An ivory wall, have you seen it? There
As we travel on the road, together'd
Shadows flit at twilight
We will not be of them vespers.

Failing in confinement,
I built it. Where were you?

John Wieners

is love the next best thing to imagination? do we, lacking the latter, settle for the former and, finding this too denied, fight over the crumbs?

david mydans

Introduction

transliteration through metamorphosis.
ideally 'twould be _auf_ _italien_.
my experience does not range that far.
it does this. a writing
similar to _la vita nuova_
in a modern idiom.
the technic is similar.
the form in unchanged but
by the rigors of time.

Part One - The Undead Count

dating is unnecessary.
i bid you welcome.
what music they make.
i bid you wolfbane.
for lack of direction,
foreshadowingly,
i bid you wolfbane.
unawares.

uncontemptuous of past,
i am on the make,
nor do i succeed.
for process nor product.
a construct of days,
the elaborate design of years.
chronos, when first conceived,
no more metaphoric,
in the sense of a long poem,
than the fact that it,
she, was
part of a chronic process
first incarnate.

in the first section, i state the timelessness of the relationship and forewarn the lady who causes my distress of my soon to be revealed inability to accept her will. in the second part, i state the purpose of the current work and my lack of awareness of said purpose (she, if not a lover, then at least a poem) when the experience was at hand.

"and asking to be rescued from

the pain you had become."

card on a silent silver screen.

at this point, the work resembles

a silent film. these are cues in the script.

and this is the card making

the form less pure.

a letter sent her.

updated perspective in flashback.

an organic cathartic from the land of the
ludicrous eaters.
he walks again by night.
pilgrimage (PIL-grim-AZH-e)
saturday return to beacon hill.
the sights and smells of phillips street.
life is a process, not a product.
the experienced chef will
be able to work with spices he has failed with before.
the ingredients of the former
having a particular taste
at a particular development of taste buds
juxtaposed and developed:
yesterday's corned beef hash can
taste today like a deep fried fresh
cod in a batter of guinness stout and stone ground flour.
what does all this mean?
ask dante. beatrice.

be a trichē.
what is trichē? i don't know
the choice is yrs from a selected
list of my choosing which you can
expand if yrs is not among.
jack spicer has lent me the wonders
of his native martian.
the twenty five year old poet schoolteacher
wenching at boston university.
the classic example, sieg freud,
of post-marital promiscuity.
parts, meryl, of this letter
exist in poetry alone.
the message is one of tone.
<u>grapheo</u>. it feels so fine.
i wish i could write poetry in greek.
flows from a joy in communicating again with you.
i never did know you as an artist, he says reminiscently.
was too infatuated

as a youth in boston in 1968.
david's in the kitchen, he ain't got no shoes.
that is where the similarity ends.
i'm in the living room
without the tombstone blues.
david is painting his light fixture
with a pale purple:
four parts dioxidine purple cum two cadmium red deep,
seven parts gesso.
a touch of vermilion.

(are there two "l"'s in vermilion,
meryl,
as in vermicelli?)

winter returned today to vermont.
a foot of snow while i was in boston
with david, more today as i return cum thumb
as am stranded duke manti style
thirty miles from home in a bar in a valley,
snowed in.

you're laboring under an illusion.

tell me something that is not an illusion.

you can be in my illusion

meryl

if i can be in yours.

my illusion is labor.

(a synthetic cathartic?)

in poetry and in life

what is the difference

between synthetic and organic?

Part Two - Renfield

spectered out again,
oxford hotel desolate monday night
rock band, ten people
and in walks a specter.
jesus, shit
if she didn't look like you.
sitting touched
in next day's kitchen.

casts in sand order one
to go out on the road.
bring to life an old edict.
(he will out on the road
for you
five yearly).
berkeley beatrice,
ribbons of highway,
taco stands, and stuckey's
mark the route i will rumble to your door.
a legend marked in cheeseburgers.

the ninth section is divided into three parts. in the first part i am sitting in a bar inflicted with visions of the lady to whom this work is dedicated. in the second part a woman much alike in appearance to my lady walks into the bar. in the third part i am much effected the next day by this experience. the tenth section is divided into two parts. in the first part i state that it is my fate to now go in search of the woman i love. in the second part i state my intention to obey the will of fate.

admit to then

and

accept fate,

that it makes no exceptions

not even you.

when yr time comes,

you will not make it happen.

of its own will,

you will off to san francisco (in this instance)

or wherever else.

you act without knowledge

of the fate of others.

"i have decided that you are

my fate and have travelled

these many miles to find out

if i am yours."

the great trundle
then undertaken.
the trip towards
the setting sun,
site of most recent world series,
and when reaching
the point one hour earlier than destination,
as one reads clocks,
stopping to record it in chronicle.

held in remission
through four years of marriage,
the fifth fully
aware of
the fate's presence,
the undertaking
undertaken
as maples toned,
through red and orange markings,
autumn's arrival.
no mosquitos
remain alive in brandon.
across eastern states, the mississippi
st. louis' arch. into
and across the continental divide
as it snowed there
and hailed in denver.
hailed the last leg of the journey,
to her home in san francisco.

not as remote as,
nearly six years to the
day from
initial acquaintance on
beacon hill.
not as remote as
was perception
of our fatality
at date
beacon hill,
long even before
marriage's conception.
the boss led into
and out of
wedlock,
just as surely as
he
led you to the spot
to which i now wend.

we met, saw yellow
sub in fall boston.
then our fall,
home to bed, pack yr bags,
move in before thanksgiving,
out just in time
to be memorialized
on memorial day.
winter together,
summer alone.
(it would have been easier in reverse.)

returning in the fall,
you had yr own flat then,
no need to call,
you didn't.
the flood and he wept.
i could today draw you a roadmap of the cracks in
the ceiling of our apartment on phillips street.
high atop dan z square.
and he wept
clear until winter
and wed.
and wore then
for four years
a long cloak.

Part Three - Mina Seward Harker

ten hours
out of her bed and board,
her chronicler
coming again to the page.
fills his spirit with the years
delights in resolution.
with solace.
as one returning winter evening to stove side
daily tremors awash on the
jacket covered hook
by the kitchen door.
lights on now.
warm in a house
admired from hilltops
across the gulf for the warmth
it must contain.
as one home at last
determines shortly to finish his task
and be done with her
for the present.

forget the partridge
had there been any need for that
i'd have gone towards pear trees instead.
and turtledoves
have less to do with
scorpios three
than i with partridges.
must be then that all
this
has little relation to christmas.
no gifts are expected.
no santa claus.
nothing expected, nothing lost.
costing no more than a generator
which could burn out some-
where
up in wyoming.

generator light came on just
out of salt lake city
just to prove that
something else was burning.

down one step as between
foyer and hallway,
yr tepid glance.
the past flowing in images
through conversation.
these looks have no past.
she knows what its like
sleeping with someone,
unemotionally,
so she claims,
someone worshipping her.
the car died,
someone said there was significance in it,
three thousand miles hence
on yr doorstep.
only she knows what its like.
only he knows
how good it felt
when david, in victory,
walked hand in hand to the peace table,
with goliath,
setting nothing,
and each went home to his own land,
fighting nothing.

no one enjoys writing poems.
no one enjoys winning.
no one enjoys losing.
there is no need for any of them.
the trip undertaken for
and culminated in pleasure.
yet lasting only hours,
or days,
unawares of images
unrelated to that feeling,
that monday night make love
for the first time in five years
feeling.
the depth of her body,
going through each other,
once figurative
once literal.
nothing is begun, nothing ended.

the loudest bed in san francisco
specially brought in for the occasion.
(she bought the smallest bed she could find.
to murder desire.)
like a coffin in the catacombs of carfax abbey
i am buried in you.
yet unseen
the bedsprings herald
announcing
something new in the world
of the real.

it was at exactly that moment

that i realized,

orgasmically,

that

the holy grail is a

gastank.

the chances that the girl you go out and pick up on the streets is a triple scorpio are one in one thousand seven hundred and twenty eight.

that sure was some slot
i chose
for my jackpot.
everybody gets one once.

comings and goings.
time comes for leaving
as it does for coming.
this love lasting
five days is long enough
for the page.
the body and spirit not sure.
that for which the journey
is obtained.
satisfaction in quest realization
for the time being
as important as life realization.

sticking yr head out
yr bedroom door
as if asking for a cup of coffee,
this way you spoke,
asking if i'd like to live out the fantasy.
to its extreme.
as if in sleeping
on her twin bed,
bellowing springs in announcement
to all interested,
she drinks my heart from the holy grail.
these legs
this skin
not a same cell remains,
each regeneration lends her farther
in spirit and flesh
no longer
in each cell regenerated
child in boston

or seen as loved child.
each new cell
into which sinking deeper
(the tremors her flesh create
are cleansing)
surrounds a similar form.
a being and feeling the same.
comings and goings
i came and went.
no lives were changed.
none moved.
no child was born or conceived.
plans and promises none.
we will, i hope, again.
in spring
or that or the one following.
for the spirit,
presently at peace,
no more remains to be said.